Hope Without Faith:

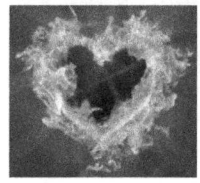

How to Ignite God's Supernatural Blessings Upon Your Life

By Evangelist Janice Robinson

Copyright © 2013
By Janice Robinson
Hope Without Faith: How to Ignite God's Supernatural Blessings Upon Your Life

Printed in the United States of America
ISBN 978-0-9894026-7-5

All rights are reserved solely by the author. The author declares that the contents are original and do not infringe on the rights of any other person.

No part of this book may be reproduced in any form except with permission from the author. The views in this book are not necessarily the views of the publisher.

Unless otherwise indicated, All Scriptures cited in this book are from the King James Version of the Bible. Copyright (c) 1973, 1978, 1984 (year) by Biblica.

Autograph Page

Autograph this book to someone who needs to be ignited with the hope of our Lord Jesus Christ.

Preface

I have been thinking about writing this book for more than seven years. God gave me the title in April 2004 in Florida. So, I began writing, and after about 10 pages, I stopped. I began to pray. I asked God why I was writing this book. I had a job and was already busy with paperwork. I had lots of excuses, but God didn't let me rest easily about writing the book.

When I lived in Staten Island, N.Y., in 1999, I met a young lady who was looking for a teacher to help with her book. Her name was Wanda Burney and she was a member of my church. Someone told her about me. We met and soon became friends.

I had no experience writing books, but Wanda and I prayed a lot; then we went to the library to research writing books. We worked on an outline for her book and set about editing her work to the finished product.

Unfortunately, I moved from New York to Florida before Wanda's book was finished, but I always remembered what she said as we got closer to the end of her book: "One day you will write a book, too."

In December 2011, I went to my hairdresser Michelle Baker and the desire to write my book was stirred up again. After getting my hair done, I was headed home when I noticed a new Christian bookstore, Java & Jesus, on Montrose Street in downtown Clermont, Fla.

I was tired and wanted to go home, but God had something else in mind. I heard God's voice tell me to stop at the bookstore, so I parked my car and sat for a few minutes, but I eventually obeyed God's command.

Java & Jesus was filled with inspirational books. As I walked around and shopped, I struck up a conversation with the female bookstore representative. I told her about Sean Cort, a member of my church who was a publisher and author of Christian books.

She gave me the bookstore owner's name and told me to call her and share Sean's information. Later that week, I called the owner and told her about Sean. Sean later called to confirm that he'd heard from the owner and they'd decided to organize a workshop for new and aspiring authors at her store.

I was excited and surprised to hear what had progressed from my brief stop at the store. I had only wanted Sean to sell his books at Java & Jesus, but God had something else

in mind. Sean ended up inviting me and six other people to his writing workshop.

Sean told us everyone has a story to tell. Those words inspired me to get serious about what God wanted me to do: share my testimony of His unfailing love and faithfulness in a book.

I hope readers of this book will find hope and inspiration from hearing about how God has increased my faith in Him as well as helped me and my family find joy despite our struggles and disappointments.

Acknowledgments

This book is dedicated to my family, both natural and spiritual.

To those who have gone on before us: my late beloved mother, Rosa Lee Robinson, born May 5, 1922, to the late Rev. and Mrs. Willie Allen of Norman, Fla.; my late beloved sister Helen Motley; and my brother the late Robert Robinson and my Aunt the late Claudia Allen.

To my two sons: Tory Robinson and Jonathan Robinson, your unconditional love, guidance and understanding have been "wind beneath my wings." Your encouragement and belief in me helped me to finish this book.

To my siblings: Dorothy World, Mary Robinson Associate Minister, George Robinson, Lois Callway, Shirley Hill, Andrew Robinson, and a host of aunts, nephews, uncles and cousins, you are all a gift from God to me and my sons. I am blessed to have all your support in the writing of this book. May God continue to bless you and keep you safe.

I am also acknowledging my pastor, Bishop Chris Dutruch, his wife, Julie Dutruch, and family for their ministry and desire to bring the Word of God to life in our lives year

after year. May God bless my pastor and Celebration of Praise church family. You all mean the world to me.

I am also grateful to my prayer partners, Gloria Goldstein, Pastor Estelle Lynch, Pastor Thomas Lynch, Evangelist Diane Williams, Pastor Rita Marshall and Nancy Burke. God has always guided us to pray for others and believe that those prayers would be answered. I hope this book will bless the people of God and forever bless my family.

CONTENTS

Chapter 1.	Nothing Like Family	Page 1
Chapter 2.	"Bread When I'm Hungry, Water When I'm Thirsty"	Page 15
Chapter 3.	"He's an On-time God; Yes He Is	Page 21
Chapter 4.	A Way Out of No Way	Page 25
Chapter 5.	The Still Small Voice	Page 31
Chapter 6.	God's Helpers on Earth	Page 39
Chapter 7.	God, My Waymaker	Page 45
Chapter 8.	When God says Go	Page 55
Chapter 9.	The Prayers of a Righteous (Wo)man Availeth Much	Page 69
Chapter 10.	Children Are a Heritage From the Lord	Page 75
Chapter 11.	My Father is Rich in Houses and Lands	Page 81
Chapter 12.	Restoring What the Locusts Have Eaten	Page 93
Chapter 13.	Holding on To God's Unchanging Hand	Page 101
Chapter 14.	Sowing Seeds	Page 107
Chapter 15.	Just Trust Him	Page 111

Chapter 1

Nothing Like Family

I have five sisters and three brothers. The nine of us, from oldest to youngest, are: Helen Motley, who has since passed away; Dorothy World, chairwoman of the Women's Day and Pastor's Anniversary at Second Mount Baptist Church of Panama City, Fla.; Mary Robinson, an associate Minister at Bethel Holy Church in Newark, N.J., (her pastor is Bishop J.H. Williams); myself, Janice Robinson, one of the founders of the Singles Ministry King of Hearts Singles Ministry at Celebration of Praise Church in Clermont Fla.; Lois Callway; Shirley Hill, an usher at Lily Baptist Church; George Robinson; Robert Robinson, also deceased; and Andrew Robinson.

We grew up in Montgomery, Ala., where we attended Catholic school and church. Later, we transferred to public school and attended the St.James Baptist church next to our home where we could just walk around the corner to church.

My father was an ambulance assistant in Alabama. He traveled a lot from county, to county, so we only saw him when he could get time off from his job.

My mom stayed home to take care of all her children with my Aunt Claudia there to help her. Caring for nine children was a big job for my mom, but she made sure we all had enough food, clean clothing and that we knew God.

We lived about a mile from the Catholic school and walked to school each day. When we transferred to the public school, it was about the same distance. We enjoyed going to school because we had many activities to choose from — music, cooking, sewing, soccer, baseball, football, swimming, drama and singing.

During my high school years, some of my sisters and I used to attend the school football games, which started early evening and would last into the early part of the night. My mom trusted us to go and come home as soon as the games were over. However, our aunt had her own agenda. Before it turned dark, she would get on her bike that had a large light she built onto it. She wanted a big light, so she would not have problems seeing at nights, since we had so few street lights.

In contrast to my mother, my aunt was very strict with us girls, but not so much the boys. She did not want my sisters talking to boys or boys walking us home from school. She was afraid we would get ourselves in trouble with boys, so when the games were over, Aunt Claudia would ride her bike to the school to follow us home, shining that huge bright light in our faces. We were so embarrassed in front of our classmates.

When I returned to school the next day, my classmates had written a song about Aunt Claudia. As I approached the school grounds, the students were singing "Lordy, Lordy Lordy, Mrs. Claudia, you sure don't treat me right."

It was embarrassing for me because the Robinson girls were the only ones who had to leave the games early, instead of going to the Whopper Burger House to eat and talk before going home. My older sisters had a 9 o'clock curfew. If they were late, Aunt Claudia would ride her bike to get them home, too.

All the girls were unhappy with Aunt Claudia's attitude

about not trusting the girls but trusting the boys. Our mom was somewhat in agreement with her because she had to raise us by herself without my dad.

One night, all of my older sisters went to their school game and returned early that night. I was asleep and so were my older sisters. My sister Lois told us that night when Aunt Claudia went looking for them, she was unaware they were already asleep.

That night, there was a loud noise at the door. My mother was afraid to open it. When she eventually did, there were four police officers at the door. They asked Mom if she had seen anything unusual in the area. She told them no, that she hadn't seen or heard anything around the house.

They told her two men had just escaped from the local prison and were sighted in the area. The officers told my mother to call if she saw any surprises. Lois said our mom checked all the doors and windows and verified all the children were in the house safely.

She looked out the window and didn't see Aunt Claudia's bike and grew worried. Suddenly, there was a knock at the door around 10 p.m. With the news of the prisoners, our mom was now even more afraid to open the door. There was another louder knock. Then she heard Aunt Claudia's voice and opened the door.

"Where are those girls?" Aunt Claudia asked as she came through the door.

"They are all in bed asleep," my mother replied. "They came home early tonight."

"I've been chasing them most of the night," Aunt Claudia said.

"Look in their rooms and see," Mom said. "They are asleep."

"Then who was I chasing?" My aunt asked.

My mom told her what the police shared that night — that two prisoners had broken out of jail. Aunt Claudia had an incredulous look on her face when she realized she had been chasing two prisoners around the neighborhood on her bike with the huge light, which probably made them afraid to stop.

Later that night, my mom called the police station and was told the prisoners had been caught down by the river dock, not too far from our home. When we heard the story, we were glad Aunt Claudia was safe, but we laughed for days.

Aunt Claudia did not come to get us from school for a whole week. We were glad. It took her quite some time to get over how she chased two prisoners who could have been armed with weapons, or that they could have used her to break into our home. We knew Aunt Claudia had a good heart and that she was only looking out for our well-being.

I had a great childhood. I was raised in a loving family. We all loved each other and God always provided everything we needed. Mom and Aunt Claudia took good care of all of us and made a wonderful home for us.

We had a large piece of property. Our chores included taking care of the fruits and vegetables in our yard and across the street on the land that was our farm. We planted seeds, watered the fruits and vegetables and watched them grow into a harvest for our family.

Our crops included apples, figs, oranges pears, pecans and plum trees; pomegranates, watermelons, blueberries, blackberry bushes, corn, string beans cabbages, okra, collard-greens, squash, butter beans, tomatoes and sugar cane. In addition to raising chickens, my mother made her own butter, bread and even ice cream, including my favorite flavor, vanilla. We had plenty of food to eat and share with our neighbors. It was fun growing up during

that time.

When I was about 5 years old, I remember my mom being sad all the time. I asked her what was wrong. She told me Dad was going into the military. I didn't know what that meant, but I knew it made Mom sad. Dad was gone for a long time, but my sisters and brothers knew where he was and when he was coming home.

My next door neighbor also went into the military with my father. I did not see him for a long time. His wife, Bessie Lee, and my mother were close friends. I loved Mrs. Bessie. I would help her clean her house because she could not do it by herself. When our father returned home, we were happy to see him and his friend, Mrs. Bessie's husband, Mr. Preston.

Mrs. Bessie's husband started drinking after he came back from the Army. Many times, he would beat Mrs. Bessie. She was afraid of him, so she did not call the police. I frequently asked my mother to call on her behalf. When she did, they would not sign for him to go to jail.

I pleaded with Mrs. Bessie to send her husband to jail, but she said she was afraid. I prayed to God to send him away if he didn't stop drinking. After many years, he had to go to the hospital for drinking and smoking cigarettes. Mr.

Preston had to have both of his legs amputated because of the poor lifestyle choices he made. Instead of leaving her husband, Mrs. Bessie stayed, taking care of him until God took him home.

As my sisters and brothers got older, things began to change in our home. My mom grew sad again. She would not tell me what was wrong, but I knew it was bad. My father started drinking and smoking while he was in the military, just like his friend, Mr. Preston. Mom didn't like that because no one in our home drank alcohol.

As the years passed, I became aware of what alcohol could do to a person and his mind after leaving the military. We all loved our Dad, but did not like it when he drank alcohol. He became a different person, not the man we knew as our father.

My mom and aunt tried to get aid for my father, but he refused to get the help he needed to make him better. One day, our father left home. We were all sad when he left. Our home went through a time of sadness. A part of us was gone. We have looked everywhere, but have never seen our father again. Due to my father leaving home our mother had to go to work and provide for her family.

My brother Robert was age 18 when I saw the same sad

look on my mother's face as when my father was with us. By then, I was 8 and old enough to understand what alcohol was. Robert came home drunk one night. My mother was dealing alcoholism again.

I was angry with my brother because I knew he was going to leave the house just as my father did. As my brother got older, his drinking got worse. He eventually left on his own, moving to New York City where my sister Helen and her husband William Motley now lived.

Robert moved in with my sister, hoping to get better. He went on to finish classes and became certified as an X-ray technician at Staten Island Hospital, where he got a good job and was doing well.

After many years, we found out our brother started drinking again. He went to get help many times, but kept returning to drinking. I missed him, so much so that I asked my mother if I could go to New York to see him. She did not want me to go so far away because I was only 12.

I told her my sisters Mary and Helen and Helen's husband, William, would take good care of me. She allowed me to go to New York. I was happy to go see my brother because I thought I could save him from what my father had gone through.

I was not sure what to expect since he left home at 18. My sisters were happy to see me and I them. We discussed the good times, when my brother was going to school and working to take care of himself throughout his years living in New York. Somewhere he had made poor choices and failed to correct them to change the course of his life.

One day, Mary and I went to look for my brother. He was staying with other people who also drank alcohol. We did not know the exact house where he lived, but we knew the area where the house was. As we were walking down the street, we passed our brother. My sister said, "There he is."

I asked where, and she said, "He just walked past you."

I did not recognize my brother. Neither did he recognize me or my sister Mary. We called out to him and he still did not recognize us. My heart broke again because it reminded me of my father when he drank alcohol.

Robert finally stopped. We hugged and I cried, asking him why he'd left us and why he was still drinking alcohol. He was shocked to see us, especially me. I used to fight with him frequently because I hated when he drank. He would not listen to my mother and played hooky from school.

Robert tried to stop drinking and seek help, but he always hung around the same people who drank alcohol. I tried to help him, but I had to go back home to school. I did not want to leave him, so I prayed and ask God to help him. After I finished high school, I ask Mom if I could go back to New York for the summer and help my brother Robert get off alcohol.

It was hard for my mother to let me go, but she always knew that I had a heart to help people since I was a little girl. She saw things in me that reminded her of her parents, Pastor Allen and his wife. They were our grandparents who died before we were born. They were born in Florida and moved to Alabama where my mother was born. I don't know a lot about my grandparents, but I am searching an area where they lived and may have pastored a church.

My mother decided to let me go to Staten Island, N.Y., and live with my sister Mary. She knew God would take care of me and keep me safe. It was hard to leave my mom, sisters and little brother Jackie. My little brother cried a lot after I left. He wanted to come with me.

When I arrived in Staten Island, it looked a lot different than when I was there years ago. There were many more people there and it didn't look like where I grew up back in Alabama. The first thing I wanted to do was look for my

brother Robert.

Mary and one of her friends helped me look for Robert. When we found him, he looked worse than when I saw him five years ago. He was drinking every day and sometimes he would sleep in cars because he had nowhere to stay. Robert didn't want to stay with my sister or my brother or seek help from anyone.

I began researching alcohol addiction. I discovered it is a disease and if you don't get help, it will kill you. My brother needed a lot of support. He had given up on life at a young age.

One night, Mary came home and told me Robert was dead. I could not believe what she said. I began crying and tried to leave the house to go see him. I blamed God because I knew He said in His Word that if I prayed and asked anything in His name, He would do it.

It took me a long time to ask God's forgiveness for blaming Him for the loss of my brother. God gives us free will and we have to make the wise choices for our lives. Later, I found out my brother died of alcoholism, but it was hard to believe. The police found him in a car close to where he lived. However, the doctors said he would have died sooner due to the erosion of his liver, which was caused by drinking alcohol for a long period of time. When my brother died, he was age 23.

Chapter 2

"Bread when I'm hungry, water when I'm thirsty"

When my son Jonathan and I moved to Clermont, Fla., from Staten Island in 2003, we arrived with little money, no friends, but an abundance of faith. My son, age 13 at the time, and I did not know anyone in Clermont, so when times got tough, we had no one to turn to. With no income, we relied on our "Jehovah-Jireh" God to be our provider when we sat down at the table to eat each day.

One particularly rough day, we prayed and blessed the food we could not see. We trusted God even though there was no food on the table. We left the apartment for about two hours. When we returned, there was a knock at the door. It was our next-door neighbor, Lisa, a Latina woman with long black hair and a big smile. Though we had just met her, she arrived with food, pots, pans, plates, forks and spoons. She said if we needed anything else, to just knock on her door, any time.

God had answered our prayer. We believed in faith that He would provide food and He had provided much more. My son and I hugged and cried together. We were so grateful that God had used our neighbor to bless us. She didn't know that we didn't have any food. She thought she was just being a good neighbor. She was living out the Scripture to "…love thy neighbor as thyself."

The next day, there was a knock on the door again. It was Lisa. She invited us to go to church with her family. She attended the old Celebration of Praise Church on Highway 27, where I would end up becoming a member years later. Those two knocks on the door by Lisa changed everything and boosted our faith in God.

The Bible tells us "Faith cometh by hearing the Word, and

hearing by the Word of God." What we cannot see in the natural realm, with natural eyes, must come by faith. Hebrews 11:1 tells us that **"Faith is the substance of things hoped for, the evidence of things not seen."** As God's people, when we read these words and not trust Him, are we living in unbelief?

Despite all the miraculous signs God has given us, both in Scripture and in our own lives, many people still do not believe in Him. When we turn our lives and our needs over to Him, we truly believe that through faith, He will take care of every area of our lives, but we must believe.

We need look no further than the Psalms to find confirmation: **"O taste and see that the Lord is good: blessed is the man that trusteth in Him." (Psalm 34:4) "But I am like a green olive tree in the house of God: I trust in the mercy of God for ever and ever." (Psalm 52:8)**

When we put our trust in God, He hears our prayers. He blesses us according to our needs, often using people, such as my neighbor, Lisa, to have mercy on the poor; and in the end, rewarding them for blessing His people. **Psalm 41:1 says "Blessed is he who considers the poor: the Lord will deliver them in time of trouble."**

God says **"The meek shall eat and be satisfied: they shall** praise the LORD that seek Him: your heart shall live forever." (Psalm 22:26). As we seek God through our trials and tribulations on this earth, He will rescue us from the "snare of the serpents." The Word of the Lord says "I will rescue those who love me." (Psalm 91:14).

Problems and trials increase our endurance and trust in God. Endurance develops strength and character in us. Character strengthens our faith, our confidence and expectations of our salvation. God loves us dearly because of our faith in Him. Through the Holy Spirit, He fills our hearts with love. (Roman 5:2,5.)

As Christians, we need to speak to our "mountain" situations and believe that they will be moved in Jesus' name. Jesus gives us power to believe that all things are possible (Hebrew 11:6), but without faith it is impossible to please Him. We need to speak positive words to the negative situations in our lives, trusting that God will make the change. We need to believe that whatever we ask for in Jesus' name, it shall be done.

As we increase our faith in God, He will give us what we ask for in His name, according to His will. God says if we have faith as small as a grain of mustard seed, we can speak to the "trees" in our lives and they'll be uprooted. Faith in God gives power, strength and boldness to Christians.

Isaiah 55:11 says "So shall my word be that goeth forth out of my mouth: it shall not return unto me void, but it shall accomplish that which I please, and it shall prosper in the thing whereto I sent it." We should always trust in our Father and obey the voice of the Holy Spirit. God wants to bless us, but we need to learn to wait and trust Him while we're waiting on Him. He knows our needs better than we do.

Chapter 3

"He's An On-time God, Yes He Is

We were living on Staten Island on Sept. 11, 2001. My son and I awoke late that morning for school and work. I returned my car back to the dealership because I was having financial hardship, so we had to take the bus to my son's school.

After arriving at my son's school, I stayed on the bus to meet his grandmother, who was working at a voting station on Staten Island. Since I did not have my car, she allowed me to drive her car to work that day at P.S. 306 Ethan Allen School in Brooklyn, N.Y. It took me from 8:10 a.m. to 8:30 a.m. to get to work. If I had taken the bus and ferry boat to work on that day, I would have been on the No. 1 train around 8:45 a.m. that morning. This would have put me right in the middle of the terrorist attacks on the World Trade Center that morning.

My son's father was in the World Trade Center when the planes hit the towers, but he and other employees got out safely. When I got to work, one of the teachers came to my classroom and told me two planes had hit the World Trade Center. I desperately tried to get to my cell phone and call my son's father, but most people could not reach their families because their cell phone services were out.

As I was praying, my son's father answered his phone. He did not know who I was. I screamed out to him. He said people were jumping from windows and he could not move from the front of the building across the street from the World Trade Center. I continued to talk to him, urging him to leave the area where he was to be safe.

"Run! Run, as fast as you can, and keep running and don't stop!" I said. He ran. I did not hear from my son's father again until around 8 that night. Later, he shared that he could not remember where he had run to during that time. He was not hurt, but in a state of shock and disbelief over what had taken place on that horrifying and sad day in the history of this country.

Chapter 4

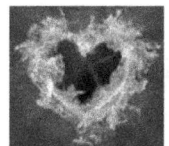

Making a Way Out of No Way

A Staten Island resident for more than 28 years, I worked for 20 years as a school teacher in Brooklyn, another borough of New York City. After graduating from college with my bachelor's degree in Early Childhood Education and History in 1984, my son and I moved from our small apartment in Staten Island into a house. I would later marry in 1995 after returning to college and completing my master's degree in Special Education in 1986. In the middle of the fall semester, my sister Helen, who suffered from sickle cell anemia, became very ill.

Helen and I were very close. We lived in the same duplex on Staten Island. She lived on the second floor and I lived on the sixth. My brother George also lived close by and we both helped take care of Helen. My mom lived in Alabama with my other sisters and brothers.

Helen's husband, William Motley, and their daughter Constance Motley; my sister Mary and brother George, were the only family members who lived in New York. My mother had taken care of Helen most of her life. Now, I felt it was my turn to take care of her because we lived so close.

Helen had suffered from sickle cell since she was a child. Sickle cell is a debilitating disease in which the body makes abnormally shaped red blood cells. There is no cure for sickle cell. When her white blood count took over her red blood count, Helen would become very sick and weak.

She was constantly in pain, had lots of colds and her low blood count caused her to need regular blood transfusions. We were a close family, so when my sister was in pain, I was in pain, too.

Helen eventually passed away December 7, 1988. My

mother was still alive when she died, and we all took it very hard. I struggled with my sister's death for many years. During that time, I was pregnant with my second child, and there was not one night that I did not cry. I had lost my sister who was my best friend. I loved her very much.

After giving birth to my son, I decided to leave New York and move to Atlanta where my sister Lois lives. I was very sad and lonely and thought that moving closer to my mother and family would help me to feel better. I found a job as a teacher. I was paid once a month and my income wasn't enough, which made it hard for me to keep up with my rent and bills.

I became depressed and decided to return to New York with my two sons. I felt sad about leaving my family, but it was hard to survive on a monthly paycheck with two children, so I moved.

After I moved back to New York, I stayed with my brother-in-law, William Motley, until we found a house to rent on Staten Island. That's when our struggles began. We began moving from house to house each year because the owners would lease to us for a year and we were unaware that their homes were in foreclosure. We moved about 17 times over the course of about 15 years. In winter 2000, it became a challenge for us to find a place to rent.

Throughout all our challenges, my sons, now ages 29 and 15, remained brave. They prayed with me, telling God, "If you are who you say you are you, then you will not let us fall."

We eventually found a house, but we were competing against three other applicants. We needed a place to live urgently. Our furniture was in storage and we had to give up our keys to our current home that very day.

With no place to go, we went to our church. We prayed and asked the pastor if he could help us. When the owner called and said he chose us as his new tenants, we knew that God had heard our prayers. We shared the news with our pastor, who then sent about five men to take our furniture out of storage and deliver it to our new home.

New Year's Eve 2002 found us in a safe, warm house giving thanks to God for His love in our time of need. When we put our hope in God we can trust Him to supply all our needs through His riches and glory.

In His Word, God promises us, **"Verily, verily, I say unto you, Whatsoever ye shall ask the Father in My name, He will give it you" (John 16:23)**. In Psalm 84:12, God tells us **"O Lord of hosts, blessed is the man that trusteth in Thee."** Jesus tells us in Psalm 37:3, **"Trust in the Lord, and do good; so shalt thou dwell in the land, and verily thou shalt be fed."**

When we choose to do right in God's sight by faith, we have made peace with Him because of what Jesus Christ our Lord has done for us. Our faith in Jesus Christ has brought us into a place of high privilege and we can confidently and joyfully look forward to sharing God's glory.

Chapter 5

That Still Small Voice

My family and I began to attend church regularly. We were grateful to the pastor for all his help as well as the people who moved our furniture. I joined the church choir and put my youngest son in the church's daycare. As a way to give back to those who had helped me in my time of need, I volunteered to help the teachers organize their classroom, strengthen the curriculum and any assist with anything else they needed.

During 2000 to 2001, my life spiritual life began to change. God began speaking to me in dreams and visions. I didn't understand what they meant, so I got quiet and waited to hear what God was saying to me. Sometimes, He would speak with a small voice and sometimes with a loud voice.

I was never afraid, just curious about why He was speaking to me. Often, I would gaze up at the stars to see if I could see God, hoping He would give me a sign of how to find Him when I needed Him.

Then in 2001, I received a sign. One night, my son Jonathan and I were upstairs in the computer room. I looked out the window and in the sky saw a bright light. It was so bright it was hard to look at. I called Jonathan to the window. We both saw a huge bright cross in the sky.

We couldn't believe what we were seeing. The light from the cross was shining into our backyard. I asked Jonathan if he saw what I saw and he said yes. I felt the presence of the Holy Spirit all over me. I didn't want to take my eyes off the cross because I felt so much love and peace all around me.

We then called my other son Tory to look.

"I don't see what you are seeing," he said. But it was gone by that time. After it disappeared, I just sat there in my computer room on the floor wishing it could come back.

I believe the sign in the sky was God's way of telling me that He existed. God speaks to us where we are. My heavenly Father knew that I often gazed up at the sky, looking for Him in the heavens, so I believed that beaming cross was His way of reassuring me of His existence and love for me.

Time moved on and God continued to speak to me, though not as dramatic as the brilliant cross in the sky.

In November, I began smelling an odd odor throughout my house, yet I couldn't find the source. My two sons said they, too, smelled the strange odor in their room, so they moved to another room.

I eventually started coughing every day. The coughing affected my ability to teach my students. It also impacted my drive to and from work. I consulted a specialist in New York City who I had seen on television and in medical magazines.

He performed many tests, but could not find anything medically wrong with me. I became very depressed and could not sleep well at night. I struggled to wake up in the mornings and prepare for my students.

This continued for about five months. I began praying to God, crying out to Him, asking him to heal me. I asked him

to show me the source of the strange odor.

One day, I heard a small voice say "Pack." I knew it was God's voice. I knew His voice by now. I asked God, "Are you sure you want me to move again? My children will think I am crazy and they will probably want a new mother."

He said, "Pack again." I always obey my Father, so I began to pack.

My sons were not happy with me. I told them what God told me, but they still did not want to move. Six weeks of packing later, I was moving boxes from the closet in the room where my sons used to sleep. I looked up in the ceiling and saw a huge black spot in the ceiling. It smelled bad. I knew it was mold.

I called my neighbor next door to look at it and he confirmed it was mold and told us to immediately leave the house. He said the house was more than a hundred years old and the owners tried to rebuild the house themselves and didn't do a good job.

We had to leave almost all our possessions in that house when we moved. I told God: "Thank you for always giving us hope to believe you will never leave us nor forsake us."

Later on, my sister in Christ, Wanda Burney, and another sister from the church attended our women's service on a Friday night to see a female pastor who had come to minister to the women. As the minister began to sing with the music, I felt the Holy Spirit all over me. She asked for people to come to the altar, so we went and knelt down.

We were at the altar crying out to the Lord when I felt a lot of phlegm in my throat begin to flow out of my mouth onto the rug in the church. I couldn't stop it; neither could I cough. As I was calling out to God, He was healing my body from the toxic elements I had been breathing in my apartment.

The pastor said God was healing people at the altar. As she said this, I saw myself in a field of grass with a warm wind blowing over me. The feeling was so peaceful that I didn't want it to stop.

The pastor then went to one of the women who came with us in the car and asked her "What you are seeing right now?"

"I see green grass and a warm breeze blowing over me," she said.

I couldn't stop crying. She was right next to me and we both were experiencing the love of our Father. She was suffering from diabetes and it was hard for her to walk.

Later, the pastor asked all of us not to move from the altar because God was doing something with us. Some people moved, but I stayed. She said, "Some of you will go to Florida and some of you will go to California, if you believe the Word of God."

As we were planning our trip to Pennsylvania, one Sunday in church, a lady approached me and told me God told her to give me one of her cars. She said you will need it where you are going. She estimated that it would probably last me for about one year. She said she lived in New Jersey and I would have to come to her house to pick it up.

I was amazed and curious because no one knew I was moving from Staten Island and we did not know each other. I asked her, "How do you know I am moving and how do you know if I need a car?"

"I don't know," she said. "I always obey God and do what He tells me to do."

We both laughed. I told her that I knew God had spoken to her because He speaks to me, too. Her husband walked over to us and shared what his wife said God had revealed to her.

He was in agreement with his wife and I was pleased. We then prayed together outside the church. She congratulated me on my upcoming move, gave me her address, phone number and told me to pick up the car whenever I could.

I was speechless and happy that God cared about me that much to give me a free car. I did not have a car at that time because the auto dealership had recently repossessed my car. I was teaching speech therapy in Brooklyn at this time, but like most teachers, I didn't make a lot of money. I missed two payments on my car, so now I was trying to make double payments and also survive financially.

This was a tough time for me because my mother was very sick. She was suffering from a rare case of cancer. She lived in Montgomery, Ala., with my younger sister Shirley. I went home for a week to see my mother. She looked well. I had to see my mother and just "love on her." God forbid something would happen to her before I could see her again.

On January 11, 1996, on a Friday evening after work, my sister called and told me we lost Mom. My son Jonathan threw himself on the floor and cried uncontrollably. I felt sad for him. He had not seen his grandmother in a while and took it hard.

I cried myself to sleep that night. I was still in shock because the last time I saw Mom she looked good. Little did I know that would be the last time I would see her. I kept remembering before I left to go back to New York one of the flight attendants had given me two little white pillows. When I went to see my mother, I gave them to her.

My sister Shirley said Mom kept the pillows next to her in bed, and when she sat in her chair. I smiled wondering if mom liked those little pillows so much because my scent was on them.

It was very hard for us to lose Mom. To us, she was the best mother in the world. I can remember her getting us up every weekend for Sunday school. We wanted to sleep longer, but Mom was always one step ahead of us. She would cook the most delicious breakfasts to entice us out of bed. By then, my siblings and I were happy to go to Sunday school.

My mother and my sister Helen were two of the sweetest, kindest people you could ever meet. They would give away their last morsel of food if you asked. They had hearts of gold. I am at peace knowing they both loved God and had a relationship with their heavenly Father. I know they are in heaven with Jesus and one day I will see them again.

Chapter 6

God's Helpers on Earth

Pennsylvania

In February 2002, my two sons and I moved to Pennsylvania, from Staten Island. Though we moved, I still continued to work in Brooklyn as a classroom teacher and speech therapist.

My family and I packed up the truck. We had no one to help us drive to Pennsylvania. I called on our pastor one more time and shared what we needed. He promised to send two men to drive us to Pennsylvania and unpack our things.

We were grateful to God and our pastor for helping us in our time of need. We found a house in Pennsylvania, moved in and found a local Church of God. When we arrived in Pennsylvania, it started snowing before we arrived at the house. One of the men noted that there were no snow tires on the truck.

We began sliding all over the street during our travel up the mountain. We prayed hard that night and cried so much our tears froze on our faces. If it wasn't for God I wouldn't be here right now. The weather made driving conditions so dangerous that the men from the church had to stay the night at a local hotel. They risked their lives to get us to our home and we were grateful for their help.

The first week in the house I was unable to get to work because I had no one to take me to New Jersey to pick up my car. Without a car, I would be forced to walk to the bus stop. The roads were dark and scary. There were bears, deer and other wild animals in the woods. I wasn't able to walk to the bus that picked up people to ferry them to New York.

Once we settled in, Jonathan was baptized. He credited me for leading him to Christ. I was blessed to hear my 13-year-old give his life to God. We often talked about the Lord while gazing at the stars and praying to God. We used those moments to talk to God about whatever we could think about.

My older son Tory and I knew God had led us to Pennsylvania for many reasons; one was to preach the Gospel to the lost and lead them to salvation.

On Monday, it was time for work and I had no one to take me to the bus stop, so I missed work that day. I called a longtime friend named Linda in Staten Island. Her sister Brenda and her family lived not too far from me in Pennsylvania. The next day, I called Brenda and explained my situation, telling her I needed a ride to work. She said she could pick me up, but couldn't promise to do it every day.

I was grateful just for one day. The next morning, Brenda and her husband picked me up for work. We took the bus into New York then caught the train to Brooklyn. Brenda was a principal at her school in Brooklyn and I went to another part of Brooklyn to my school as a teacher.

On the way back to Pennsylvania from New York, I asked the bus driver, "Do you know of anyone who lives closer to me to get a ride to the bus with?"

He said, "Yes, and she loves to help people. Her name is

Millie Warren and she lives three houses down from me on the opposite side of the street."

He gave me her phone number, so I called her. When she answered the phone, I told her who I was and where I lived. She invited me to her home to meet her family and have dinner with them. Things were looking better.

When I got to Millie's house, we introduced ourselves, and sat down for dinner. She had two children and said my son Jonathan could walk to her house and ride the bus to school every day with her children. Millie was home from work because she had hurt her leg in the World Trade Center terrorist attack in New York City.

Millie was the fire marshal on her floor. When the first plane hit her tower, she was helping people get out of the building. Millie was one of many people who survived that day, but she had hurt her leg badly trying to get out of the building.

Millie also offered to help Tory find a job and get someone to drive him to work every day. She was true to her word. Tory found a job and Millie got someone to take him to work every day until he was able to buy himself a car for himself.

Jonathan took the bus home from school every day with Millie's children, Joey and Jessica. Once they got to Millie's house, she served them dinner and ensured they did their homework. What a blessing that was, as I got home too late at nights to cook all the time. Millie was one of the nicest people I've ever met.

Chapter 7

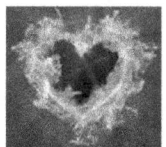

God, My Waymaker

In March 2002 on a Saturday morning, my friend Millie took me and my oldest son to New Jersey to pick up the car that a member of my church had given to me because she heard from God. After arriving at the woman's house, her husband greeted us and invited us into their home.

We discussed our lives and shared our mutual struggles throughout that year. We also ate lunch and they showed us around their home, introduced us to their pet, a talking bird that prayed and chatted all day long.

They gave me the car, a Mitsubishi Mirage, and told me what it needed to keep running. We were grateful to this family for obeying God. Their gift blessed us so much. We needed this car to travel around Pennsylvania because we could not keep depending on Millie to take us everywhere we needed to go. She had a big heart and would have continued driving us around had we never gotten a car.

After spending the day in New Jersey, we headed back to Pennsylvania. When we started the car, it sounded weak, but we trusted God that He would get us home safely. We prayed, put our trust in God and headed home.

Once we got on the highway, we were going so slow every car passed us since we couldn't get the car to go beyond 50 mph, particularly when we started climbing the steep Pennsylvania hills. The car shook as the other vehicles zipped past us, seeming to go at 70 to 80 mph. If you've ever been to Pennsylvania, you know it has many hills, curves and deep slopes. When we had to go around those curves, it felt as if the car was about to turn over.

We weren't sure if we would make it up the hills. My faith in God was still growing, so it took a great amount of courage to hold onto the wheel of the small car and trust we would make it home. I have never prayed so hard and so long to God in my life. I told Him, "When you get us through this one, I will do anything for you."

Tory was just learning how to drive and wanted to help, but I thought it was too dangerous to allow him to take the wheel. He talked constantly to encourage me. I was so glad I had him with me because I could not have done it by myself. I know God had His angels with us at all times because the car was old and small and we were risking taking it on this 50-mile trip.

When we finally arrived home, it took me a while to get out of the car and go into the house. I kept thanking God. I was so happy to see the house and Jonathan again. When I tell this story to people, they can't understand how we made it home safe. It took us about four hours to get home that night, a journey that would normally have taken an hour.

It was hard to walk and climb the stairs to get to my bed when I got out of the car. This was another hard test for us, but God was true to His word that says "I'll never leave you nor forsake you."

Millie was so glad to see us. She was worried that it had taken us so long to get home. I told her and her family about our scary ride from New Jersey to Pennsylvania and how we prayed together on the way back.

Millie wanted to know more about the Bible and our faith walk with the Lord, about how we put all our trust in Him. Millie and her family were Catholics, but she was interested in learning more about my faith, the Bible and understanding the Holy Spirit. I became Millie's teacher in the study of the Word.

She was hungry for the Word. I was fulfilling God's purpose and calling in my move to Pennsylvania. On Saturdays and over the phone, Millie and I studied the Bible together. She had many questions, which I did my best to answer. Millie was a fast leaner who enjoyed studying the Bible. She encouraged her children to study, too.

Millie was still recuperating from her work-related injury, so she had more time to read and study the Word. Due to my work schedule, it was hard at times to stay the course, but I gave her Scriptures to read and wrote questions for her to answer. When we met, we had major discussions about the Bible and how we should live by the Word.

Some Sundays, I invited Millie and her family to my church, Paradise Assembly of God Church. While her family enjoyed the service, they said it was very different from their church. Sometimes they expressed confusion at the differences in teaching styles between the Catholic Church and the Assembly of God. They continued

attending the Catholic Church while studying the Bible.

In August 2007, Millie and her family moved to Tampa, Fla. She and her family accepted Jesus Christ as their personal Savior. Millie was baptized at her church The Crossing in Tampa on April 22, 2012. She is now joined at church with her two children Jessica, Joey and her oldest daughter, Alicia, her husband Sergio and their children. Millie and I still discuss the Word over the phone. I feel very fortunate that God connected me with Millie and her family and that I chose to obey Him and ministered the Gospel to her family.

I am grateful to God for always being there by our side and using people as His hands in the earth to take care of all our needs. When you need Him, just call out to Him. He will always hear you because He never slumbers nor sleeps, and He will never leave you nor forsake you.

On my first day of church, I met a young woman named Gloria Goldstein. I had gone to the altar for prayer. Somehow, she knew I had endured a lot in my life. She prayed a beautiful prayer over me, asking God to heal me of all the pain and suffering I had gone through in my young life. Gloria and I became friends and prayer partners. We prayed often for our families, standing in the spiritual gap for them and their well-being.

Jonathan, Gloria and I sometimes ministered to people in the community. We would meet them in church or in stores and pray the sinner's prayer with them. Some accepted Christ into their lives and repented from their sins.

If you are reading this book and don't know Christ, please pray these words: **"Lord Jesus, I believe you are the Son of God, that you died on the cross for my sin, then rose again three days later that I might have eternal life. Please forgive me of my sins and come into my heart to live. I promise to commit my life to you, and follow all of your ways. Amen!"** (Acts 2:21)

Many of those people we met in the community came to church to give their lives to Christ. This was all new to me because I had never led anyone except my sons to the Lord. It was very hard for me to go up to a stranger and tell them about God and ask them to give their hearts to Him. I love God and I knew God, but I didn't share the word of God with my brothers and sisters.

I began to feel at peace in my life again after all the years of moving from place to place not knowing where our lives will end up. It is a horrible feeling not knowing whether you are going to be homeless with no place to live. We learned that we had to put our hope, faith and trust in God

who truly loves us and gave His life on the cross for our sins. We never gave up on God despite all our trials, troubles and disappointments. Trust God and believe all things are possible to them who believe. (Mark 9:23)

After living in the house for three months, we decided to move again because the house had a smoke-like odor. We prayed and asked God to help us get the strength once again to find a place to live. In the meantime, we moved in with a member from our church. Of course, my sons were unhappy because we were moving again.

God used me to pray with the church member because she lived alone and was sometimes depressed because her family lived in other states. Though we are struggling, God can still use us to help others and share our faith, love and time.

I continued to travel on the bus from Pennsylvania to New York into Brooklyn to my school. Each day was a struggle to get back and forth to work. In the winter, I always had to clean the snow off my car by myself around 2:30 in the morning before I could drive and get to the bus stop by 3:30 a.m. If I missed the bus, then I was late for my class in Brooklyn. A tardy would not look good on my professional records.

Each day, it got harder and harder to live in Pennsylvania and enjoy life. I cried out to God, asking Him where I should go and what He wanted me to do with my life. In April 2002, God directed me to go on a 40-day fast. I thought about it for a while, asking God to confirm that He wanted me to go on the fast.

I didn't hear from Him anymore because when God speaks sometimes He only speaks once then we have to obey Him. I chose to obey God and I began my 40 days of fasting at the beginning of April and continued on into May. I chose to fast from midnight to 5:30 in the evening due to my late arrival back in Pennsylvania.

Excess food on my stomach would cause me to not be able to rest or have a good night sleep. It was very hard for me at the beginning of the fast because after traveling for long periods of time and teaching all day I didn't have much strength left in my body to function at the level I was used to.

I prayed and cried out to God every day and it became a little easier in my daily life. I became stronger in my faith. I read the Bible every day, which gave me more knowledge, wisdom and understanding of what God was trying to tell me. The more I read the Bible and sought God, the more I understood what He was trying to tell me.

He was trying to show me the best path for my life and my children lives. The more I stayed in the presence of God, the more I built up my hope, faith and trust in Him more than I had ever done in my life. After finishing my fast during the month of May, my life became clearer and I saw that the challenges that I'd faced were good for me. They built up my strength, character, faith and hope in Christ.

The travel meant a long day for me. Commuting 100 miles into New York from Pennsylvania meant I had to be on the bus at 3 a.m. and ride for about two, sometimes three, hours to work. After working all day, I had to take the long journey back home again. I got home between 8 and 9 p.m., even later in the winter season when it snowed.

Chapter 8

When God Says Go

I grew tired and unhappy as the days passed. It seemed as though I had no time for myself. The only time I felt complete was when I went to church and worshipped God. I prayed and asked God: "Is there more for me to do in this life?" He didn't answer me right away, but I continued to pray and believe that He would speak to me in His own time.

One particular Monday, it was time to return to work again. I loved teaching my students. This was the joy of my life. However, this day was a special day for me in my classroom because I knew God was up to something.

I was teaching my class how to read when one of the speech teachers came to my classroom. She had a lot of art papers and some books for my students. She said the students had to do an art project for the annual speech picnic at school. My class had to choose a state that they would like to fly over and visit and complete an art project to display outside at the speech picnic.

I asked the class to choose five different states then vote on one they wanted to visit. One of my students named David used to visit his grandmother in Florida every summer, so he chose that state. All the students voted to visit the state of Florida.

As the students began their projects, we researched Florida. We read books, discussed Florida, looked at magazines to find pictures of Florida and drew pictures of Florida. We took the artwork and started our project by choosing American Airlines as the airline that would fly us to Florida.

Many of the children had never been to Florida, so this was an exciting project for them. As we began our project, the children made an airplane, calling it American Airlines.

Next, they made a colorful rainbow in the sky. They drew clouds. They created streets with people, with cars and trucks traveling to Disneyland. They made palm trees, grass and orange trees, with oranges on the trees and on the ground. They sketched pictures of little children with happy faces.

We were proud of our project and the children's hard work. On the day of our event, all the children from District 19 in Brooklyn who received speech therapy hung their pictures for display. It was beautiful to see the creativity and wonder in the blossoming work of the children.

Little did I know my students were painting a picture of my future. As it became closer to the end of the school term in June, life began to look brighter for my children, our future and me. At the end of June, I heard God say "Go to Florida."

"Lord, they have hurricanes and tornadoes there. I didn't want to go to Florida," I responded.

But, I heard God speak again: "Go to Florida."

I knew He wanted me to go to Florida. In June, I started packing day and night. I was looking forward to living in Florida. In July, my youngest son and I went to Florida to look for a house before we moved there. That's when the struggles began again. The real-estate person I was supposed to meet called me as we were traveling to Florida and said the homes we were supposed to see were not in good shape.

We didn't have anyone to pick us up from the bus station, so I called one of my friends in Pennsylvania to see if she could help. She has a brother-in-law who agreed to pick us up from the bus station and take us to the time-share villa where we were going to stay for five days.

My friend's brother in-law picked us up and drove us to the villa where we would be staying. We only had enough money to last us three days, but we knew God had a plan. So, Jonathan and I prayed and asked God to help us in our time of need. The person who picked us up from the bus station cooked a big meal, enough to last us for two days. He dropped it off at our villa, then took us to look at some homes in Clermont, Fla.

We were excited and happy about the plan God had for us in Florida and providing the help we needed. We stayed in the villa for five days and paid only $99, plus we got to use the establishment's amenities for free because of a connection with a church member back in Staten Island. What a blessing. My son and I played miniature golf, went

to the pools and enjoyed other exciting areas at the villa. We didn't want to leave when it was time to go. I recalled looking up at a large pine tree at night on the golf course and crying out to God, "Is this where we are finally going to live?"

God didn't answer me and I didn't ask him again. The next day when we were supposed to return to Pennsylvania, we didn't have enough money to buy both tickets. We went downstairs and a woman at the villa's front desk asked if I wanted to see some of the new villas for sale. I told her I was leaving to go back to New York. She offered to pay me $75 to spend 90 minutes on the tour.

We were so happy because it was enough money to get us back to Pennsylvania. We went on the tour and returned in time to get a taxi to the bus station. We made it just in time for the bus because this was our last stay at the villa. We went back to Pennsylvania with great memories of Florida. After arriving home, my best friend Gloria was excited to see us and, as always, she prepared a great meal for us.

Gloria was always a big help, not just to me and my sons, but to anyone who needed help. She loved God and always prayed for people, especially at the altar at church where she would lead people to Christ. I told Gloria I wanted to go shopping for clothes for my move to Florida. I was sure

God had a plan for me and my family to own a home in Florida. I sensed Florida would be a place of peace, joy and relaxation, somewhere where we could stay in one place instead of moving every year.

There were other challenges with Florida. Jonathan, who was 14 at the time, didn't want to move away from his father and friends. One day he left the house and didn't tell me where he was going. I got worried.

Tory was ending his night shift at work when he spotted Jonathan and bought him home. He had gone to a friend's house down the street from us. When Jonathan came home, I asked him how he felt about the move to Florida. I shared how God spoke to me about moving to Florida and starting a new life for us. I explained to him how hard it was for me to travel back and forth to work each day and never spending enough time with him and his brother. Still, I understood he was tired of moving and wanted to be near his father.

Our flight was scheduled for the next day. There was a knock at the door and it was my sister in Christ, Gloria. She said God spoke to her and told her to drive us to Florida.

I was so happy because my son was still angry about moving to Florida and Gloria's decision gave me peace of

mind. We packed much of our things into Gloria's car, leaving all our furniture behind until we can get it later. Unfortunately, I had already paid for my airline ticket, which cost about $500. It took several months to get a refund from the airlines, but after much wrangling they finally gave me the money.

We were off to Florida for a new beginning and new life. Gloria was quite handy at reading a map and we talked a lot about our new life and prayed along the way. When we reached Virginia, Gloria called a good friend of hers, Sang, who paid for us to get a hotel room and rest.

Sang took us all out to breakfast the next morning and we prayed for him and thanked him for his generosity. As we continued the trip, Gloria called her brother, Willie, and told him we were on our way to Florida and he invited us to stay at his house with his wife, Paula. He cooked dinner for us and we actually ended up staying in a hotel for the night, which Willie generously paid for. Meanwhile, Paula shared a lot of information with me about Florida's school system.

Gloria was happy to see her family. We thanked and praised God for their generosity. After arriving in Clermont, our final destination, we stopped to eat at a local Denny's restaurant. The first person we met, our waitress, Mary, shared her story about her boyfriend, her little baby and not being married. I asked her if she went to church and she said her boyfriend did not want to go to church. I told her I had just moved to Florida, did not have a car, but when I got one I would pick her up and take them all to church. This seemed to make Mary very happy and we all prayed at the table then hugged and said goodbye.

Gloria insisted that we stop at the supermarket before we head off to our new apartment. "You need food to last until you get a job," she said. She bought us food to last us a few days since she had to head home to Pennsylvania to get back to her job as a bus driver on Monday.

We arrived at our new apartment to find it locked. We could not get in. The woman from the management company, Stephanie, told us she would put the key in the microwave. Instead, she had locked the door. We didn't have a place to stay.

We asked someone for help to get in. They tried, but had no luck. So, we prayed then went back to check on the apartment and noticed that the door was open and the key was in the microwave. My sons and I were happy to be in our place to rest, so we could get a good night's sleep and I could get ready to go out the next day to look for a teaching position.

The local school system said they did not receive my information, though I had submitted it several times via computer. By this time, school had begun in August and I was still without a job. I had submitted my résumé, degree certifications and license to the Lake County School system, but they had nothing.

It was the same with my references. My former principal, Ms. Arthella Addei, sent a letter to the county three times before it was received. But I did not despair; I had to trust God and believe that if He told me to leave my home and go all the way to another state to live He would provide. I had to trust God with all my heart and lean not to my own understanding.

I prayed every night and I told God that whatever He wanted me to do in Florida I would do it. The next day, I decided to use the computer in the rental office clubhouse. When I arrived, there were children working on the computer. Though I needed to use it badly, the children also needed help, so I decided to assist them. As I was helping them, we began praying together and asking God to help them with their schoolwork.

Later, their mother came in and I shared the details of why I moved to Florida. Her name was Jennifer and she had two children in elementary school in Clermont. We became

friends, knit together because we both needed food for our families.

Jennifer had a car, but I didn't, so she often drove me where I needed to go. One day, we went to a local church and asked for help with food for our families. The church asked me to fill out a long application and I waited to hear what they could do to help me. One of the assistant pastors called me into his office and gave me two Wal-Mart gift cards for $10.

I was thankful, but I had no vehicle and $10 worth of food wouldn't last very long. He asked me why I had moved to Florida. I shared my story about how I had faith and trust in God, that I believed that all things are possible to them who believe.

"God told me to go to Florida," I said. "He knew what I had to go through to follow Him and obey his word."

The pastor sat back in his chair. He seemed amazed that I had left a good-paying teaching position to move more than 1,100 miles with no guaranteed job, no family and less than $500 in my purse.
God always tests His children's faith to see if we trust Him, to see if we believe that He is God Almighty and owns everything.

So there I was with no way to get to the store. We only had a little bread and some cold cuts left. The next day, my son and I ate the remainder of our food. We had only a pitcher of water left in the refrigerator. A day later, Jennifer called and told me she went to the local church to ask for help. They told her about a place called The Neighbor Faith Center in downtown Clermont. She asked if I want to go with her. I said yes and off we went.

There was a long line and we had to wait. As I was standing there, I began to pray for the people who were standing in line with me. I heard the voice of the enemy say, "Look at you now; you moved here and you have no job and no food."

I told satan, "One day, I'll be back and I will help feed these people."

That night, my son and I sat down at the table and prayed to our heavenly father to bless the food that we could not see and believed God that He would provide for His children. The next day, my neighbor knocked on my door and shared that she had found two elementary schools in Clermont who had posted jobs online. She asked me select a school to apply for a job. I told her Pine Ridge Elementary is the school where I will work. I thanked my neighbor for her and her husband's generosity to me and my sons during

our hard times.

I called Pine Ridge Elementary school and spoke to the secretary to apply for the teaching position. She asked me if I could come in that day, complete paperwork and go to the county office and to be fingerprinted.

September 3, 2003, was my first day of work at Pine Ridge. It was also my first interview with the principal, Cindy Kinat. Before the interview, we had a long talk about the new school and how the builders were still working on the building while school was in process. We discussed how busy she was getting the building ready for the new school term. She said the builders were still working to finish up while class was already in session. She said she felt like a chicken with her head cut off.

Principal Kinat had a wonderful sense of humor and we talked about how she loved her job and loved working with children. I had a wonderful interview with Principal Kinat. She was pleasant to talk to and made me feel at home. We laughed together and I shared why I decided to move from Pennsylvania to Florida. This was one of the most beautiful days of my life.

I felt the hand of God on me that day. He gave me favor, peace, joy, strength and His love that passes all

understanding. The next day, I went to work for the first time. It wasn't easy because I still didn't have a car. I took a small bus that takes seniors around Clermont and I had to wait for a long time, which made me late for work.

Miss Kinat e-mailed the entire school and asked who could offer me a ride to school and to take me home. I received so many e-mails that day that I didn't know whom to choose. Two teachers, Mrs. Anita Olsson and Mrs. Myrna Meyers, volunteered to drive me to work and home every day until I bought a car.

I always shared the Word of God with them and my testimony of how God took care of me on my journey to Florida. We shared great times together talking about our jobs and families. These two women stepped up and offered me their time and help when I was in great need. What a blessing.

I thank my Heavenly Father for giving me the strength to endure the challenges and trials that my son and I had to go through to follow Him. As we continued to trust God and acted upon His word, He "rebuked the devourer" and opened the windows of heaven for us.

Chapter 9

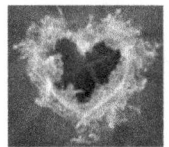

The Prayers of a Righteous (Wo)Man Availeth Much

After living in Florida for three months, my older son decided to leave Pennsylvania and come to live with us in Florida. During this time, my dear friend and sister in Christ, Gloria, decided to move to Florida, too, so she met up with my son Tory to travel together in their separate cars.

As they were traveling down the mountain in Pennsylvania around 2 a.m., a car ran into my son Tory's car twice and pushed his car into the other lane. It was a blessing that no other cars were coming at that time. My son's car was not totaled and he didn't have a scrape on him, but he was very shaken up.

The driver of the car that hit my son suffered a diabetes attack and passed out. The police and ambulance arrived to take the man to the hospital and examine my son, but Tory refused to go to the hospital. He just wanted to go back to Pennsylvania and not travel to Florida, but Gloria convinced him to continue on. They prayed and Tory continued driving in his battered car. We still don't understand how he made it to safety.

That same night, the Holy Spirit had awakened me early that morning, just before the accident. I got on my knees and I prayed for traveling mercies for Tory and Gloria. I stayed on my knees for hours praying for God to keep them safe on the highway until they arrived in Florida. When they arrived in Florida and I saw my son's car, I couldn't believe my eyes.

I didn't know he had an accident. They hadn't called me because they didn't want to worry me, but I had felt something wrong in my spirit. God woke me up to pray and trust Him with my son's life.

As we build our hope and faith in God, He gives us the

strength to endure situations that are out of our control. There are some things we can't bear, so we must trust God to take care of our loved ones because He can care for them much better than we can. Praise God because He took care of Tory and Gloria and brought them to Flordia safely.

Jonathan and I were happy to see Tory arrive safely and have him live in Florida with us. We were all together again. We had no car, but we knew God would provide for us. We had hope and faith in Him.

While teaching at Pine Ridge Elementary, I met a new kindergarten teacher named Terry Powell who was hired after me. We became friends and I helped her settle into her new assignment. I told her I needed a car to get back and forth to work and she took me to a dealership.

I found a red car that I liked. We took a test drive. I was happy with this car because it was almost new, very clean and the price was right. When I sat down with the salesman, he looked at my credit and said the score was not high enough to buy a car.

Mrs. Powell said, "Pray and don't worry. You will get the car tonight and drive it home."

It was getting late and Mrs. Powell had to leave because it

was almost 10 p.m. and she had to travel a long distance to get home. I was a little afraid because we had no way of getting back home.

I had to truly believe God again and use my faith and my hope in Him to do a supernatural miracle for me tonight because we did not have a way home. I prayed with my two sons. The salesman, Mark, came back into the room. He asked, "You are a teacher?"

I said, "Yes I am."

He said, "We can't disappoint the children because they need their teacher to be on time. We are going to work something out for you, so that you can drive your car home tonight and get to work on time for your class."

The car was a 2001 Mitsubishi Mirage. I was speechless and amazed at how good God is to His children and those who trust in Him. Sometimes we lose hope in God but, we need to have faith to know that God will not leave us. He is always with us when we are in trouble.

The salesman drew up all the papers and gave us the keys to the car. We thanked him for taking a chance on us and trusting us. He said, "Good luck and enjoy your class, your students and your stay in Florida."

We praised God all the way home. I could not wait until the next day to tell Mrs. Power that her faith encouraged me to truly trust God that night. When two or more people are praying and they both are in agreement for the same thing, this causes God to go into action and work it out for them. I was happy to have my very own car to drive to work and take my family out to dinner.

My storms were passing over. I was beginning to live again. I gave God thanks for pulling us through.

Chapter 10

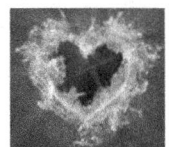

Children Are a Heritage From the Lord

Meanwhile, Tory was taking a test to become a teacher's assistant to work in the Lake County school system. He passed, receiving the highest score in his group. Tory landed a job at East Ridge High School in Clermont working as a teacher's assistant.

The principal at that time was Mrs. Arial Coles. Tory later went back to college part time to complete his degree in Technology and Education. The school administration department was very pleased with Tory's work ethic and how well he worked with the students and his peers.

East Ridge High was the same school Jonathan was attending as a 10th-grader. This transition was good for them because Tory could drive his brother to school every day as the bus did not pick up students where we lived. This was all new for Jonathan and, at times, like most teenagers, high school was not fun, especially since he was in a new state and school.

Jonathan, especially, missed his Dad and his friends, but he got support when he became good friends with Michael Willis, who helped him adjust to the new school. Michael help Jonathan get through some tough times during his high school years, through talking, going to church, reading the Bible and discussing the Word. Jonathan learned how to forgive, put the past behind him and move on to the future and enjoy life. Both teens had struggles, as most youth do, but they were able to get past them and graduate from high school. Their friendship continues today and they still encourage each other through the Word of God.

Jonathan joined the Army in 2007, earning honors by saving two of his comrades' lives while deployed overseas. He chose to run through bullets flying all around him to get a medic to attend to his fellow soldiers.

He always wore a green bandana around his head that had Psalm 91 written on it. He said God had him in the palm of His hands because he trusted God and His Word. Jonathan believed by faith that whatever situations he encountered, God was with him.

Michael went to school to become a dental assistant part time and work part time. He also married a beautiful young lady named Jamie. They are both going back to College, with Michael attending Agricultural Engineering.

Jonathan will be getting out of the military soon with his new wife Tiera Robinson and will attend college on a scholarship. He has decided to major in business/law and open up a boys and girls club to empower and transform the lives of young people in our communities.

I am very proud of both Jonathan and Michael for choosing to better their lives instead of making the wrong choices like some teenagers do. God gives us choices and we have to make the best decisions for our lives. As mothers of teenagers, we have to stay in prayer and agree with other parents who trust God that He will work on behalf of our children. I stayed in agreement with Michael's mother, Cassandra Willis, daughter, Melissa Willis, and their father, Michael Willis, Sr., concerning my son from the day we met them in 2004 at their home.

They loved Jonathan because they recognized his needs: He was separated from his father and friends and had just moved to a new state. God blessed me to meet the Willises and fellowship with them during a time of need in our life. We all attended the same church, Celebration of Praise in Clermont. This was also a blessing because we fellowshipped together at church and at our homes. This family has stayed in our lives since we met back in 2004 until now. They remain concerned about me and my sons and our well-being.

We are blessed to have people like this family stay in our lives for such a long time and continue to care about us. This is only because of God's favor. May they forever be a part of our extended family.

In 2004, when we moved from the Village at South Lake Apartments, Tory transferred from the High School to Minneola Elementary School, just minutes away from the new house where we moved. Tory loved East Ridge High School, but he couldn't resist the short drive time to his new school. He has worked there for 8 years. He loves his school, enjoys working with the children and helping them with their homework after school. Tory also enjoys working with his colleagues and the school administration.

In 2012, Tory's professional peers voted him School-

Related Employer of the Year. He was invited to the Lake County School award ceremony April 13, 2012, to receive his award. He was very excited for this wonderful award because it meant his colleagues and the administrative staff recognized his dedication and work ethic with the children.

Tory now says he is thankful he moved to Florida. He put his education on hold for a while because of financial issues, however, he plans to return to college to finish up his education. He is happy, enjoying his life and looking forward to a new beginning here in Florida.

Chapter 11

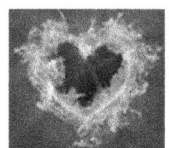

My Father Is Rich in Houses and Lands

After working at Pine Ridge for about eight months, I found out one of my student's parents was taking a real estate test to sell houses. She was nervous about taking the test, so I told her I would pray for her that everything would work out. She passed the test and offered to show me some houses.

I didn't feel I was ready to buy a house at that time because we had just moved to Florida and I had not saved enough money for a down payment, however, she was so excited about obtaining her real estate license that I went with her just to see some of the homes and the price ranges.

She took me to Orlando to meet a mortgage broker to see if I could afford to buy a house at this time. I was getting excited because I had never bought a house before. When I arrived at the mortgage broker's office, she didn't inquire about my background right away. She wanted me to talk to senior citizen Dorothy Davidson who had purchased a house through the broker.

Dorothy no longer wanted to live in the house she had bought. The real estate company asked me to go to Dorothy's house to talk to her about keeping the house for her to live in. Dorothy had lost her husband a year earlier to cancer and she missed him very much. I discovered she lived in my community and that the house was only a short walk from my apartment.

That Sunday when I came home from church, I thought about Dorothy, but I didn't go to see her. After leaving church the following Sunday, I heard the voice of the Holy Spirit say, "Go see Dorothy."

I said, "OK Lord." I dropped my bag on the couch and went to see Dorothy. As I was walking to her apartment, I asked

God: "What am I going to say to this lady?" But he did not answer me. When I arrived at Dorothy's door and knocked, she opened the door. I told her my name and that God had said to me, "If you want that house, it's yours."

She had a big smile on her face. She said, "Come in, sit down. Tell me more."

She looked so pale and sad when I first saw her, but now she began to get some color back into her skin. She told me that a friend was trying to take her house from her and put his name on the mortgage. I told her we would petition God and pray that He would hear our prayers and intervene for her to remove the man's name off her mortgage, so she could move into her house.

We sat down for tea and Dorothy began to talk about the Prayer of Jabez in the Bible. She knew everything about Jabez's story. I found it very interesting because I had never heard about the story of Jabez. We talked for hours and hours about Jabez and how blessed he was. She had a copy of some of the pages about Jabez's life and gave it to me. She told me to read it every day.

Dorothy blessed me. I knew God wanted me to meet her and for us to be friends. Her husband had gone on to be with the Lord and she had no other family in Florida. They had all passed away except for some cousins and their children. I will never forget that afternoon I spent with my new friend, Dorothy.

She invited me to stay for dinner and talk some more. As the week went by and Sunday came around again, I went to church and the pastor's sermon was about the Prayer of Jabez. The Pastor preached about Jabez's life and why his mother named him Jabez. I could not wait to tell Dorothy what the pastor had preached about at the service. I went to her house after church and we talked about Jabez's prayer again and how God has made a way for her to live in her house peacefully.

God wanted me to be Dorothy's friend and take care of her because she had no one to take care of her needs. Dorothy and I became good friends. We went to church together, shopped and visited with each other when I was off from work. We both lived in the same development, only minutes from each other, so it was easy to go and check on her if she needed anything.

In April 2004, Dorothy decided to move into her new house in Minneola. She was so happy. The real estate broker, her friend, my son and I helped move Dorothy's furniture into her new house. She thanked God for sending me to help her move into her home. We all prayed and I blessed her home, asked God to always keep Dorothy safe and give her strength to take care of herself when I was not around.

I was still living in the development. My lease was up in August and we didn't know if we wanted to lease another year or find a home to buy. I never did hear from the real estate broker again, so I began to look for houses on my own. We prayed to God and asked him: "Is this the place where you are going to give us our first home? If it is, we thank you in advance and believe that the things we hope for is the evidence of things not seen."

I was hoping to buy a house, but God's plan was different from mine. One day in August 2004 as I was visiting Dorothy, she said there were some new homes behind her development and we should go to see them. Dorothy, my son and I went to see the homes. We were very excited. We went in to look at two models. The first one was a one-story home. As we walked through the house, I fell in love with the double sinks and the island in the center of the kitchen.

The house had four bedrooms, a living room, family room, kitchen, dining room and two bathrooms. Dorothy sat on the couch and we prayed. Dorothy prayed to our heavenly Father: "Please give this house to Janice and her sons."

Afterward, we went back to Dorothy's house, had lunch

and talked about our home and how God was going to make a way for me to buy that house.

Our lease was up August 31, 2004, and the development did not renew our lease, so we had to quickly look for a house. During that time, we were coming out of our fourth hurricane and the weather was still rainy and windy outside. However, I still had to look for a place to live on that day. I searched and searched all over Clermont and did not find the type of house I was wanted.

As I was turning off Highway 27 onto Citrus Tower Boulevard, the wheel of my car refused to move. I continued driving down Highway 27 feeling confused about what was happening. I did not know where I was going at that moment. I then I realized I was in Minneola. I heard God say "Go back to where you prayed."

I turned off Highway 27, which was close to Dorothy's house. God was telling me to go back to the development where Dorothy, my son and I prayed. I went to the model house where Dorothy and I prayed. The manager was inside, so I asked him, "Are there any homes for rent?"

The manager said there was a house down the street in the cul-de-sac, so I went to see the house. There was a "For Rent" sign out front. As I pulled up my car to the garage door, I began to weep and weep because it was the same model that Dorothy my son and I had prayed in.

I was overjoyed and blessed knowing God was preparing the way for me to believe that He could give us this house to be our home. I will never forget that moment for the rest of my life. Nothing had ever happened like that in my life. I walked around the house. I could see the double sinks in the kitchen. I knew it was the same house. I blessed the house, claiming it for my family.

I thanked God for Dorothy's prayers and showing me this development. I couldn't wait to share the news with her, to see her face and talk about the goodness of God.

When I went to see Dorothy, she said, "Janice, do you have good news?"

My answer was "Yes. God is going to give my family and me this house for us to own for the rest of our lives."

Dorothy and I danced around the house with excitement and joy in our hearts. God had heard our prayers. He had given us what we needed, which was a place to lay our heads. We were so grateful to God for this house. We wouldn't have to live in a shelter or on the streets because we didn't know anyone in Florida. When we went back to our apartment, the U-Haul truck was packed and weather conditions had improved after the hurricane. We prayed and had the best night's sleep we had in a long time.

On Monday, when I returned to work, I had no calls about meeting anyone at the house to sign the lease. No calls came the next day either, so I contacted the real estate agency during my lunch hour. When I asked why no one had called, the person on the phone said he was sorry no one had contacted me and he would meet me at the house around 4:30 p.m. that day. If he were late, he said he would send someone to let me into the house.

I arrived at the house at 4:30 p.m. sharp, but no one was there. I waited about 35 minutes then a man and his wife showed up. They let me into the house. I walked around recalling the model house that Dorothy and my son walked through. It brought peace to my heart that I felt the presence of God. When I came back into the kitchen, the man and his wife were there with three other people. The original person I was supposed to meet arrived with his wife, too.

Numbers are significant to God as evidenced throughout the Bible. I study numbers and each one has a meaning. At first, there were three people, including me. Three is significant of the Father, Son and Holy Spirit. Six is the

number of man. Seven means completion and eight means new beginnings.

This was our new beginning in Florida and the new home that I and my sons were going to own. Everything we'd asked God for He was bringing it to pass in our lives because we were in total agreement with His word. We had hope and faith in God and His Word. We believed this was one of God's miracles and that's why He had told me to go to Florida. When we hear God's Word, we must obey Him. It can change our destinies.

During the week of September 20, 2004, I returned to the house and met with the realty company. We signed the lease and I gave him a check for two months' rent and a month of security deposit. I asked him to hold the check for 10 days until I got the money from my 401(k) account. He agreed. We signed the lease and he gave me the keys to the house.

I was so overjoyed I could not speak. I wept and wept until I could not cry anymore. I went back to my apartment to share the wonderful news with my sons. When I arrived home, they knew I had good news for them. We thanked God for his supernatural miracle in our lives. Sometimes we don't know the battles people are going through. Trusting God and holding on to hope can guarantee us a victory

through Jesus Christ our Lord.

On September 24, 2004, my sons and I moved our furniture into the house. We blessed it and gave it to God and left everything in his hands concerning the house and the land. I left the house for about two hours and when I returned, they had almost everything in place. I could not believe my eyes marveling at how hard they must have worked to accomplish this. It told me how much they appreciated all the hard work I had to do to find a place for us to live with our almighty God leading the way.

When I returned to work on Monday, I received a phone call from the realty company. One of the supervisors said they would not hold my checks until the money from my 401(k) was deposited into my account. They would not allow us to move into the house.

I told to the supervisor that the person I met with accepted my checks in good faith knowing that I would receive the funds from my 401(k) in 10 days. She repeated that she was not going to wait and we had to return the keys to the house. As she was talking, I was silently praying.

I told her we had already moved into the house and we were not moving out because we were not told that we could not move into the house. The next day, I took my

eldest son's hands and we prayed and asked God to resolve the situation because we knew that this was going to be our house.

The woman from the realty company called my job every day that week, but the secretary kept telling her she that she had to take a message for me because teachers cannot receive phones calls at school. She told her to call my house. She called my job one more time, but we did not hear from her again.

Five days later, I received the 401(k) money via express mail. I immediately sent it express mail to the company with a letter explaining that the person who gave us the additional time and waited for the money had compassion on us because we had nowhere to go. I thanked him for trusting I would pay for the house. God will bless him for his actions in our time of need.

As we went through these trials, we continued to trust God and keep hope alive in Jesus. It seems that as soon as we finish one trial another is on the way. Thank God we had experienced these types of trials before and knew to put our trust in God. But the next trial was around the corner.

Chapter 12

Restoring what the locusts have eaten

The house did not come with a refrigerator. The landlord had to buy one. In the meantime, we had to put our food in a cooler for more than a month. It was hard, but we managed to live without complaining. We were grateful that we had a place to live.

Meanwhile, I kept calling Sears asking when the refrigerator would be delivered. They kept saying soon, but it took more than a month to be delivered. We were glad to have it and get rid of the cooler.

In April 2010, there was a knock on my door. The person at the door informed me that the house was in foreclosure, that the landlord had not paid the mortgage in more than six months and told me to call the lawyers representing the bank. I was shocked because I had paid my rent on time every month and kept all my receipts. The landlord never called to inform me that the house was in foreclosure.

During this trial, my hope began to waver. Florida, in particular, had been hit hard as a result of the housing crisis. We were undergoing hard economic times. People were losing their homes. I had to refocus myself and regain my faith in God, to continue trusting Him even when it seemed like all hope was gone.

The housing and economic downturn wasn't just affecting Floridians. It had rippled out to people across the nation and the globe. There was nothing they could do — and I didn't even own a home yet. As I prayed for my family to own this home, I also prayed for other families to keep their homes.

When God gave me the title for this book in September 2005, I had a dream in 2002 when I lived in New York. I

heard God say "houses" three times. As the years passed, I believe He was showing me what was already happening during the tough economic times across the country, especially the housing market and in Florida. I believe the three houses represented the Father, Son and the Holy Spirit.

The people who lost their homes would get homes once again if they didn't lose hope and faith, but continued trusting and believing that God owns everything and he is a rewarder of His people. We have to pray and believe that God is alive and well and knows what His people are going through.

We have to pray, read our Bibles every day, fellowship with God and find a church home. We must also learn who Jesus is and why He died on the cross for our sins.

While we waited and checked on the status of our home, we also prayed for the owners of the house and asked God to make a way for them, even though they did not make the mortgage payments on the house. We never know what people are going through in their lives.

I stayed in contact with the bank's attorneys and the courthouse three times a week. That April, the house was going on the steps of the courthouse for sale. I prayed to

God to cancel the sale of the house. Twice the sale of the house was canceled and we praised God for his goodness, grace and mercy.

In September, we were under contract to become the owners of the house. I told my realtor that God sent us to Florida to give us this house to be our home. I shared our situation and began working with the bank to get a mortgage to buy our first home. There were challenges along the way, however, we had God on our side.

Interest rates were low and we bought our house at a good price. It was wonderful news for my family. We finally had a house of our own. On the day of the closing, Tory and I looked at each other and just smiled. He was speechless.

We did not lose our hope in God. Deuteronomy 28:8 says, **"The Lord shall command the blessing upon thee in thy storehouses, and in all that thou settest thine hand unto; and He shall bless the in the land in which the Lord they God giveth thee."**

On June 22, 2011, we took ownership of the house. God is good and He is no respecter of persons. What He did for me and my family He will do for you because that is the kind of God we serve. He is a rewarder of those who diligently seek Him and believe in His Word. I always felt

God was leading us to our new home in Florida as we looked to him to continually supply all our needs. Trials help us grow spiritually in our walk with God. My family and I have gone through a long journey to get to where we are now, but God has His own timing in the things that He has for our lives.

As we press on in the Word of God, we need to know in our hearts that we serve a mighty, powerful, loving and wonderful God. We have to build up our hope, faith and strength in God as we go through trials and tribulations. As we are enjoying our home, I am continuing to live by the Word of God through my ministry as a leader in my church, prayer warrior and as a member of our nonprofit organization Christian Manna Outreach, Inc., Men and Women of Purpose. These ministries bring the Word of God to people and help feed and clothe the needy in our communities.

God is using our board of directors – Pastor Estelle Lynch, Pastor Thomas Lynch, Evangelist Diane Williams, and myself to bring His word to people, show them His love and share His death on the cross for their sins.

During the month of March 2011, Dorothy's health began to deteriorate. She was placed in a nursing home for about five months. Over the years, Dorothy's health was up and

down. She went back and forth to the hospital over the past five years. I visited her in the hospital day and night.

She maintained her sense of humor throughout her ordeal, making the doctors and nurses laugh. She was smart and knowledgeable about everything, especially the Bible. She shared the Word with those she met, often leading them to the Lord. Dorothy and I spent a lot of time together sharing the Word and talking about Jesus. She told me many stories about her dreams and visions and I shared my dreams and vision with her, too.

I was very saddened about her health, but Dorothy would respond that she knew she was going to heaven to meet the Lord. She always talked out loud with the Lord and shared God jokes about everything. This was how she fellowshipped with the Lord ever since she was a little girl. She said it made her happy to be near the Lord.

One day, she shared a dream that she had when she was 7 years old. Dorothy became very sick and died on the operating table. She went to heaven. It was beautiful with tall mansions decorated in some of the most beautiful colors one could ever imagine. She said she saw tall angels praising God all day long. One of them spoke to her and told her she had to go back home to her mother. She said she told the angel she did not want to go back home.

"Your mother misses you," he said. Dorothy said she told the angel, "OK." When she opened her eyes, she was back on the table surrounded by doctors and nurses. She told the doctors she went to heaven to see Jesus, how beautiful it was and that she did not want to come back home.

They looked at her with amazement and later discovered that she was completely healed, so they sent her home. They never forgot Dorothy and her amazing out-of-body experience in heaven. I enjoyed listening to Dorothy's dreams and visions.

On July 14, 2011, we celebrated Dorothy's 90th birthday at her home. She loved her house and did not want to live in a nursing home. She said she wanted to stay in her own home until God was ready to take her home. On August 11, 2011, I went to see Dorothy and spent almost all day with her. She was in a good mood and did not appear sick at all. A hospice doctor came to visit her. He asked her a lot of questions and she teased him about a lot of things. They laughed a lot. Dorothy always knew how to get people to laugh and be happy.

Before I left her that day, she told me she dreamt she had passed away and her friend George was there with her. We both cried. I told Dorothy, "Don't cry. I'll stay with you." Beginning that evening, the home-care aide stayed with

Dorothy all day and night up until the time she passed away on Monday, August 15 at 10 a.m.

Dorothy went home to be with the Lord. This was a very sad day for me because I had lost my best friend. She reminded me so much of my mom because she had such a warm, kind and loving spirit. She was a wonderful human being who loved people. She loved the Lord with all her heart and soul. I hope to see her again in heaven. I was happy that she lived long enough to see God answer her prayers for me and my family to have our own home.

She inspired my life, encouraging me to have a deeper relationship with my heavenly Father, moreso than I have ever had in my life. Spending time with Dorothy helped increase my hope and faith in God, strengthening my relationship to a level beyond anything I could do on my own. When we face life's adversities, we need to have hope. We should never lose hope. We have to keep standing strong and ask God to build our faith. In prayer, we must show God how much we love Him and realize how much He loves us.

Chapter 13

Holding on To God's Unchanging Hand

I am still following, trusting and believing God for my purpose in life. I continue to provide food and clothing for those who are in need. There are so many people around the world who are still in need of the presence of God in their lives. When we turn everything over to God, we won't lose the hope that we have in Christ Jesus. **"For I know the thoughts that I think toward you, saith the lord, thoughts of peace, and not of evil to give you an expected end." (Jeremiah 29:11)**

During this time in my life, God is leading me to feed those who are in need and assist them in counseling, to help to

locate housing for families who have lost their homes in this economic crisis. I feel God wants me to help people who are feeling hopeless.

In 2006, God gave me a vision of a building. But he never said what was going to be in the building or where it was going to be located. I have prayed and believe that God's Word will not "return void" because His word is the truth. What I went through in 2003 when I ran out of food stayed with me and has inspired me to help others who may not have food to eat or a place to live. I believe my heavenly Father wants me to be compassionate, to share my story with others, to help those who have gone through or are still going through the pain of not having any food or enough food to feed their families.

I was the founder and chairperson of our nonprofit organization Clermont Christian Life Center. All the board members and I donated time to organize and set up Thanksgiving food baskets for families. Our corporation is currently dissolved due to lack of funding to execute our mission. We don't have a building, but we believe God will provide a building and all the resources we'll need to carry out his mission for the sons and daughters whom He loves very much.

When we are going through a crisis, we should always pray and listen for God to respond. We should go to church or a friend or a family member who can pray with us, believing with us for the things we are asking God for. God will hear your prayers. He is compassionate and will give you what you need.

In September 2003, I prayed with my youngest son. He believed with me in what I asked of the Lord. He had the faith to believe Jesus would give us what we asked for and He did. Our Father loves us and wants to give us what we need.

With the help of sponsors, which included Publix, BJ's Wholesale Winn-Dixie, Bravo and Wal-Mart, our organization distributed six gift baskets of food to six families for Thanksgiving in November 2011. This was our first giveaway to help people in need of food in our surrounding communities in Clermont.

This is just the beginning of what God wants for us and others -- to be His hands and feet in our communities, to reach out to help those in need. As I carry out God's purpose for my life, I will walk by faith and not by sight. What I can't see will not stop me from executing the plans that God wants me to accomplish.

God doesn't want us to give up hope, especially when things get tough. We have to hold on to our faith and trust His word that He will fulfill the plans He has for our lives. This will bring glory to God.

Tough times are not mistakes. God knows what we are going through, but when we lose hope, we can lose everything. Many without hope can feel displaced. If we lose hope, we can fall into despair and lose faith in what we are believing God can do in our lives.

During my trials, I kept hope alive and built up my faith, so I could remain strong and trust God to meet the needs in my life. It's not easy to keep your faith strong. You have to work hard to encourage yourself. You have to read your Bible daily. You have to pray and keep thanking God for giving you another day. You have to honor Him, continue to love Him for keeping watch over you and your family.

Matthew 6:33 says to **"Seek ye first the kingdom of God and all these things shall be added unto you,"** so there is hope for a better life in this world, but we have to obey the word of God and apply it to our lives on a daily basis. No matter how hopeless our situation, we must remember that the joy of the Lord is our strength. We must hope that joy will spread to our families, marriages, jobs, businesses and ministries.

When we have a relationship with God, we can readily cast our cares on Him. 2 Chronicles 16:9 says "For the eyes of the LORD range throughout the earth to strengthen those whose hearts are fully committed to him." So God is looking for people who love Him simply so he could minister to us.

God will use all things to "work together for our good." Sometimes that is to build our character, to get us to be grateful for His blessings and to strengthen our faith in Him. He will cause us to prosper and be in good health even as our souls prosper–even in a recession!

We have to stand strong on the promises of God. His blessings will come and overtake us. He will deliver us out of the poverty-enslaved life in which some of us have lived for years. As the desperate cry out, God will provide protection, deliverance, strength, hope and faith to all who seek Him and obey God's commandments.

Chapter 14

Sowing Seeds

In September 2010, I went to Bread of Life Fellowship, a food bank, to fill out an application to get food to distribute to people who were in need of food in Clermont. As I was completing the form, Mr. Mark Anthony, a worker at the food bank, asked me where I lived before moving to Florida. I told him Staten Island. I shared my testimony of running out of food and how The Neighborhood Faith Center had helped feed us.

I told him I had been looking for the center since 2005. He said the organization had moved to Groveland, Fla. I was so excited to hear they were still in operation. I went to see them in October 2011 and met with Mr. Jerry Colyer, the executive director of The Faith Neighborhood Center.

He was quite moved that I came back to visit them so many years later. I told him how grateful I was for their help back in August 2003 when my family and I ran out of food while I was trying to get a teaching job in Clermont. I told Mr. Colyer I was writing a book about my life and how I ended up relocating to Florida.

I am thankful to the staff of The Faith Neighborhood Center for providing food for me and my family when we were in a place of great need. I also sowed a financial seed into their ministry and gave them boxes of Psalm 91 books to share with those in need. The director said he was pleased to know that people appreciated what their ministry did for those in the surrounding counties in Florida.

Since 2003, after not having enough food to feed my family, it has been my heart's desire to evangelize and tell people to not give up hope. During harsh economic times, it's easy to lose hope, but I am writing this book to inspire you to never give up your hope in God. He sees all of our troubles and when we call on Him, He will answer.

When I ran out of food, I had no one to help me. I felt

alone and ashamed. You don't have to feel alone. You don't have to feel shame. Just give it all to God. That's what my son Jonathan and I did. We serve an on-time God. It didn't take Him very long to answer our prayers. We believed and didn't doubt in our hearts that God would provide us with food.

God's Word says if He can feed the birds in the sky, what more would He not do for us. He loves us and doesn't want us to suffer. Not only was sin nailed to the cross, but hunger was nailed to the cross, too. Everything was left at the cross. This is why Jesus came to this earth, to give us life and life more bountifully. We have to know Jesus' death was not in vain. He came to give life not take it away from us. God wants me to live an abundant life, without lacking anything. I have to want the same for myself. I have to have a made-up mind about my life and how I live in this world.

We are all God's children. We must know who we are in Christ and know He is Christ our King, our Lord and Savior who gave His life on the cross for our sins. God is just looking for people who will believe that He is who He says He is. He is the son of the living God and He is still alive. If I believe in my heart and mind that He is a living God, I can believe Him for anything: healing for sickness and disease, employment when I have no job, provision when I have no food, a house when I have no home for my

family, peace when I'm having problems with our children, and a faithful, loving spouse when my marriage is on the rocks.

For me to come out of poverty into living an abundant life, I have to make a choice to read my Bible, go to church and Bible study classes to learn the word of God. This will open our eyes to understanding the Bible. This will help us to study the Word at home, help us meditate on his Word and memorize and live out the Word of God in our lives.

When I allow God to work in my life and my family's life, it will change us from the inside out. We will find peace, joy, love and patience as we wait on God's bountiful blessings to come into our lives. It is important to focus on our new futures in Christ and leave our past behind. When I focus on my future, my mind is free of things in the past that take up so much space that I can't think or focus on what I want to accomplish in my future. This is why reading our Bible brings understanding and helps us make good decisions for our lives. I have to learn to keep my mind free of worry, stress and problems.

Chapter 15

Just Trust Him

"If you make the Lord your God your refuge, He will make the most high your shelter, no evil will conquer you; no plague will come near your dwelling. For He orders His angels to protect you wherever you go." (Psalm 91:9,10,11)

When trouble comes our way, we have the power to speak to the mountains that stand in our way. God gives us the strength and the boldness to stand against the enemy and all his tricks. But we need to use our faith and His power to show God that whatever the situation, our faith will always stand strong. God is pleased when He sees our faith.

Every trial that comes against God's people cannot stay because we carry the faith of our ancestors Abraham, Moses and David. As Christians, we need to put faith and hope in Jesus for everything we need in our lives. As we walk in faith, God will open the windows of Heaven and pour out blessings that you and I cannot contain. Everything we need, Jesus has already provided.

We serve a mighty and powerful God who loves us with all His heart. Whatever God has promised, we must always trust Him to carry out His Word. He is not only the God of Abraham, Isaac and Jacob, but He is your God, too.

Psalm 31:24 says, **"Be of good courage and He shall strengthen your heart, all ye that hope in the Lord."** God is saying, "Let it go and trust in me." When you tell that mountain to move, it will move from your life. When we speak to our situations, we are speaking life to our needs. No matter what it looks like, no matter how we feel, God says it's already done and everything you've lost shall be returned to you double-fold.

God says all you have to do is believe in your heart and have no doubts. Believe and trust My word and have faith in me. When we get out of God's way, it allows Him to work on our behalf and bring everything to completion. If

we put all our problems in His hands and trust Him, He will bless us so we can be a blessing to others.

If we just praise Him and worship Him at all times, He will dwell, or take a seat, in our presence. When we have fellowship with Jesus Christ, it sets the atmosphere for us to worship Him in spirit and in truth. God loves when we praise Him and show Him how much we love Him, when we give Him thanks for all He has done for us. God loves each and every one of us. He has billions of blessings for us if we just trust and believe in Him. Jesus wants us to read His words in the Bible and meditate on them day and night; get them into our minds, spirits and hearts. As we repeat them and keep them in our thoughts, then God can manifest those things that we believe in and return them to us in double-fold blessing in our lives.

God wants us to go to a quiet place where we can pray and seek Him and share our thoughts with Him. He loves when we bring all our troubles to him and ask Him to help us. God is so pleased with us when we leave everything at His feet. We are showing Father that we trust Him to take care of all our needs, instead of us trying to help Him out.

We can do all things through Christ who strengthens us. Faith is depending on God and waiting patiently for Him to work everything according to his timing. God's thoughts are higher than our thoughts. He knows everything about us. He knows how much we can and cannot bear. He does not give us more than what we can handle. If we acknowledge Him in all our ways, He will direct our paths. If we mediate on His Words, then everything we ask will come to pass. Romans 8:24 tells us **"For we are saved by hope: but hope that is seen is not hope: for what a man seeth, why doth he yet hope for?"**

God always prepares the way for His children. When we try to do it on our own, then God cannot get the glory. As we go through hard times and trials, we must have hope. But we need to learn to build up our faith and stay in agreement with someone who believes God and whose faith is strong. Deuteronomy 32:10 says if one can put a thousand enemies to flight, and two can put 10,000 enemies to flight. Just imagine what we can do when we all come together.

If we humble ourselves and pray to our Father, He will hear our prayers and heal our land. When we pray, we need to choose a place that is quiet to seek God. We must wait for God to speak to us in that quiet voice, that still small voice. When we are doing all the talking to God, we don't allow Him time to talk to us and we'll miss hearing His voice.

Sometimes, God wants to get our attention, so He can speak to us, direct our path and show us where He wants us

to go. We serve a jealous God and He wants our attention the same way we want his attention. As children of God, we need to develop our minds to be in tune with the Holy Spirit to learn how to follow Jesus' plan for our lives. He wants His children to be obedient to His words, to learn His voice when He speaks to us.

I cannot live without God. He is my everything. We must carry Him with us everywhere we go -- in our cars, to our jobs, to the marketplace, the doctor's office, even we go to asleep. He is our source, our strength, our hope and our faith. He is an awesome God, and we love Him with all our hearts and soul.

Jesus will always fight our battles and bring justice to those who love Him. We know we can always run to Him when we need Him because he is always there. He said He will never leave us or forsake us. When friends, family and loved ones are not around, we don't have to worry about being lonely. We can call on Jesus and He will show up. There is no one else like Him! He is our strength, our deliverer our defender, our Savior and our God. He is our hope, our miracle, our breakthrough and our blessing. (Deuteronomy 28:2)

He opens doors no man can close. He closes doors no man can open. He pours out blessings that we can't even imagine. He goes where we can't go and makes the crooked road straight. When we shout out to the Lord, He hears our prayers and answers everything we ask in His name and according to His will.

He is our king, our Lord, our Christ and every wall that is blocking us, He will make come down. When we come up against life's Walls of Jericho, all we have to do is shout and walk around it seven times and the barriers will come down. Shout! Shout! Shout! Seven times.

As we praise and give thanks to our God, the Holy Spirit, He gives us wisdom, knowledge, strength and power to overcome the works of the enemy. We are living in times that may cause God's people to lose hope. But we must make up our minds to sow seeds in the mist of our troubles and show the devil that we are the King's Kids and we will reap a harvest despite the famine.

We must learn that no matter what it looks like in the natural, in the heavenly realm the angels in heaven are working on our behalf. God sees everything before it happens in our lives because He is in control of our lives. Therefore, when we speak, we must do so as if it were already done. This is our hope, that we believe everything God says will come to pass.

This is a dry season, a time most of us have never experienced before and we have to come together as one people, no matter our race, ethnicity or gender, to seek the face of God, asking Him to have mercy and heal our land. God knew that we would go through this economic famine before the beginning of time. He is still on the throne and in charge of everything concerning his sons and daughters in this world. God's Word says in Roman 8:27, **"And he who searches our hearts knows the mind of the Spirit, because the Spirit intercedes for God's people in accordance with the will of God."** We must keep the faith and continue to make intercession for the saints.

Roman 8:28 promises, **"And we know that in all things God works for the good of those who love him, who have been called according to his purpose."**

As we pray, let's ask God to search our hearts for anything that is unclean in us, repent and be healed. When we do this, Jesus can work through us and in us. This will help us to become better people in the eyes of God. It is important that we choose two or more people who will pray with us and be in agreement with what we are asking of God. God honors our obedience to Him and as we submit our will to His will and He will bless us more than we can comprehend.

It is He who gives us a new heart to love our neighbors as we love ourselves, and to love all people as Jesus did when He walked the face of this earth as a human being. God lives among us, every day His spirit lives in us and we take Him with us everywhere we go. As God's light shines through us on the earth, it will draw people closer to us. They will see God in us.

We serve the highest God, the only God in the universe, the one who made the heavens and the earth. He is the Alpha and the Omega, the Father, the Son and the Holy Spirit. As we trust Him with all our hearts and souls, He will deliver us out of our personal crises and increase our faith so we believe God our Father can do this.

Man cannot do this by his own strength, only our Father in heaven, who has all power and strength to overcome the world, can do it. We must rise up and do what God has ordained for his sons and daughters to do. As God's people, we need to seek the face of God in these terrible times. From the White House to every house, we must ask God to forgive our sins, to forgive our hatefulness toward others and save us from all unrighteousness upon this earth.

We need to ask God to heal our hearts, minds, our land and our souls from the works of the enemy. We cannot live without God in this world. He made man from the dirt of this earth and woman from the rib of man. We are joined together as one and can never be separated from Him. We have to decide if we're going to serve God or man. God wants us to choose to serve and obey Him. When we obey the word of God, we will pray and wait on the Holy Spirit to direct our path.

This ensures we will follow the leading of the Holy Spirit to do what God wants us to do, instead of what we want to do in our own strength. When we disobey our Father, the windows of heaven will no longer be open over us. The "devourer will not be rebuked" off the fruit of our vine and we will lose the blessings of the law of multiplication.

We will lose the superabundance that God has promised. "Those who trust in the Lord shall never be disappointed." Psalm 103:17 says "His promises are for his children and their children's children." As we put our trust in God, and believe through our faith without wavering, God will turn everything around in your life for your good and it will bring Glory to Him.

God will supernaturally do miracles in your life and people will know that only God could have done this. As you speak what you do not see, call those things forth as though they are, believe in things that you cannot see, this builds up your faith in God. Jesus just wants to see if you will step out

on His word and trust Him. We have to be like little children to inter into heaven, God says.

When we have that child-like faith, it pleases God. It shows Him how much we love Him and need Him in our lives. In the Bible, Jesus rebuked His disciples when they tried to keep the children from coming to Him. He told the disciples to let them come and he received them in His arms.

This is how Jesus wants us to come to Him -- willing and on our own without any doubt in our hearts. When Jesus asked the disciples to follow Him, they dropped everything and followed Him everywhere as He went throughout the nations. As we pray, we must ask God to speak to our hearts and help us follow Him, being led by the Holy Spirit to trust Him. He will show us the way we should go.

As we follow Jesus and read his words every day, it will help us to live a holy, prosperous life full of joy and happiness. Jesus wants us to have the kind of abundant life like he gave Adam and Eve in the beginning. We can live that life if we follow all of God's law's and do not disobey his words. When we love each other and do good unto others, as we want them to do unto us, God can heal our land and we can live among each other with love and kindness.

God is commanding His people to live by faith and not by sight. When we walk by faith, it helps us to stay positive, not worry, not stress, not be angry and not harbor bitterness toward family and friends. It is not easy to live by faith. It is a learning process. Our actions move God to intervene on our behalf and supernaturally work everything out for us.

Romans 8:35, says **"Who shall separate us from the love of Christ? Shall trouble or hardship or persecution or famine or nakedness or danger or sword?"** No one can separate us from Christ's love -- not principalities, not evil spirits, not powers, nothing that can harm us. We are the children of the highest God and we carry His power and strength in this earth. He died on the cross and rose again to make intercession for us during these perilous times upon the earth.

We must trust God to intervene in our situation and bring hope to us when it seems like there is no hope. Faith is believing that no matter what the enemy tries to do to us, we can call on God and trust that everything will be in His control. Jesus is looking for people who have faith in Him no matter what the situation looks or feels like.

As we walk in obedience and keep the commandments of the Lord, Deuteronomy 28:2, promises that **"all these**

blessings shall come on thee, and overtake thee, if thou shall hearken unto the voice of the Lord thy God." As God's people, we should read and obey His commandments and live a holy life.

Through it all, however, we must have faith. Hebrews 11:6 tells us that **"without faith it is impossible to please Him, for he that cometh to God must believe that He is, and that he is a rewarder of those who seek him."**

BIOGRAPHY

Janice Robinson has been an educator for more than 25 years. She was a teacher in the New York City Department of Education for more than 20 years. Her dedication to the department's After School Programs was recognized by the New York City mayor's office in 1999.

Her work as an educator was also hailed by "Who's Who Among American Teachers" in its October 1998 issue. This Prestigious Educator Award was stated by publisher Paul Krouse. "There is no greater honor teachers can receive than to be recognized by former students for their excellence and dedication.

Her work as a Reading Specialist was also hailed for her Commitment and Dedication to the New York City Housing Authority Department of Community Operations for after school "Partners In Reading Program on June 21,1999

Janice holds associate's degrees in English and History, is a graduate of the College of Staten Island, where she received a bachelor's degree in Education. She continued her education at Columbia University, taking courses in Speech Pathology.

Janice says "teaching has been one of the most enjoyable experiences of my career. As an educator, I want to be an integral part of helping students achieve their success through education."

Born and raised in Montgomery, Ala., Janice moved to Staten Island, N.Y., before finally relocating to Clermont, Fla. In August 2003, she joined the teaching staff at Pine Ridge Elementary School in Clermont, teaching kindergarten for seven years.

Janice is a faithful member of Celebration of Praise Church of God in Clermont. A visionary, she is a founding member of Clermont Christian Life Center, Inc., a nonprofit corporation started in 2010 to provide mentorship and support services to at-risk people in the local community. Though the center is now dissolved, Janice continues her ministry to those in need through her church food ministry Praise Pantry, at Celebration Of Praise Church and the ministry of The Church At South Lake Buses n' Backpacks food program for the Lake County School System, and a spiritual leader of Christian Manna Outreach Men and Women of Purpose Inc., a nonprofit corporation.

www.ingramcontent.com/pod-product-compliance
Lightning Source LLC
LaVergne TN
LVHW041628070426
835507LV00008B/511